TANK GIRLS

JOHN FRANCIS HOPE

WAG BOOKS

INTRODUCTION

Not for stick in the muds!

The tank was invented at the beginning of the century, a hot, smelly, noisy, machine that was as often as not stuck in the mud. Life for the tankie has improved a great deal since those early days but, apart from the odd celebrity trip by Margaret Thatcher or Princess Diana, has remained very much the preserve of the male.

We have decided to change this and let some of our more relaxed and uninhibited models loose on a variety of machines, to get the female reaction to these huge hulks of steel. They were fascinated, of course, and wanted to explore every knook and cranny, clamber over every protuberance and squeeze into every hole. There is, as they discovered, an awful lot to play with on a tank. We choose to shoot on a very hot day and the girls as you will see, found it extremely hot and exhausting work. Some simply refused to wear the tank crew clothes they were given.

There was something about the size of the gun barrels, the calibre of the weapons and the potency of the ammunition that made these tanks of particular interest to our models. There's no doubt that getting to grips with main armament of this size made our model's day and gave them a bench mark against which so many other weapons will be found wanting.

After reviewing these beautiful examples we very much hope that the cause of feminism has been further advanced and that in time to come the all-girl tank crew will become *de riguer*. If not, then I am sure that armies around the world will consider providing at least one tank girl for each crew to provide a calming influence in the heat of battle.

To all concerned we give our heartfelt tanks.

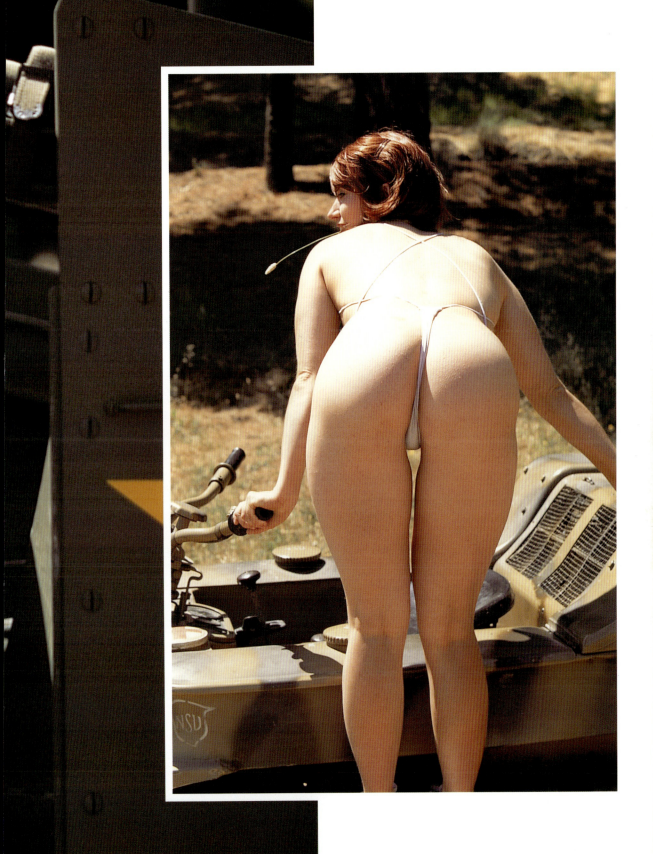

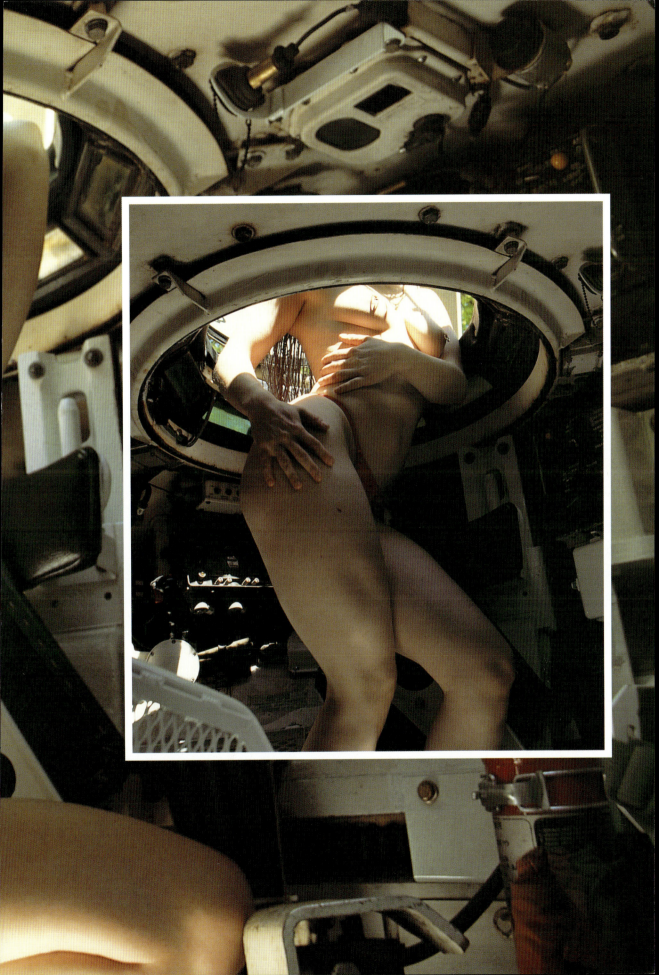

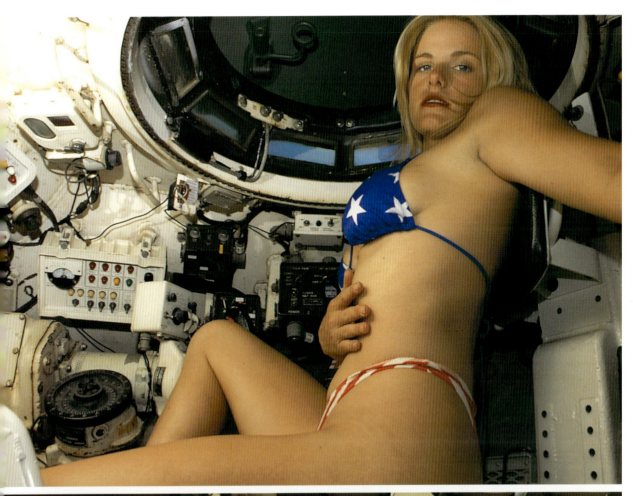

WAG Books is an imprint of Compendium Publishing Ltd
5 Gerrard Street
London W1V 7LJ

Designed by Compendium Design and Production
Printed in Hong Kong through Printworks Int. Ltd.

@ Compendium Publishing Ltd

All rights reserved. No part of this publication may be reproduced or transmitted in any form by any means electronic or mechanical, including photocopy, recording, or in any information storage and retrieval system, without the prior written permission of the publishers.

A CIP catalogue record for this book is available from the British Library

1-902579-18-6